YOUTHS

THE AGENTS OF CHANGE & DEVELOPMENT

An essential handbook to help you grow responsibly and live a fruitful life

Gatluak Dang Thoat

A Note from the Publisher

The publisher wishes to acknowledge and thank Dr Douglas H. Johnson for his invaluable help and support for Africa World Books and its mission of preserving and promoting African cultural and literary traditions and history. Dr Johnson and fellow historians have been instrumental in ensuring that African people remain connected to their past and their identity. Africa World Books is proud to carry on this mission.

Effort has been made to give credit to whom it is due. Several stories have been carefully selected from sources such as magazines, newspapers, and books written by other authors. For example, most of the stories have been retrieved from the website: https//www.moralstories.org. Footnotes/endnotes have been used to cite other sources and websites that have been consulted and used.

Unless otherwise indicated, all scripture quotations are taken from the New International Version. Copyright © 1973, 1978, 1984 by the International Bible Society. Used with permission of Zondervan Bible Publishers.

All the scripture quotations marked 'CEV' have been taken from The Holy Bible: Contemporary English Version.

© Gatluak Dang Thoat, 2020
ISBN: 978-0-6488415-4-8

All rights reserved. No part of this publication may be reproduced, stored in a retrieval system, or transmitted, in any form, or by any means, electronic, mechanical, photocopying, recording or otherwise, without the prior permission of the publishers.

This book is sold subject to the conditions that it shall not, by way of trade or otherwise, be lent, re-sold, hired out or otherwise circulated without the publisher's prior consent in any form of binding or cover other than in which it is published and without a similar condition including the condition being imposed on the subsequent purchaser.

Design and typesetting: Africa World Books

The writer can be reached at
gatluakdang24@gmail.com/dang4peace1994@gmail.com

Table of Contents

Dedication	5
Acknowledgements	7
Foreword	9
Introduction	11
Chapter One The Importance and Power of Being Young	15
Chapter Two Youth and Education	21
Chapter Three Youth and Social Responsibility	30
Chapter Four Youth and Peace and Security	38
Chapter Five Watch Out! The Devil is After You	47
Chapter Six Remember Your God While Still Young	61
Chapter Seven The Success Formula	68
Conclusion	77
About the Author	80

Dedication

To the youths of South Sudan. We are all familiar with our situation. Our nation is in deep need of the awakened minds and committed hearts of young people longing for peace, love, and cooperation. These things will allow us to catch up with the rest of the world. A change of attitude is all that we need. It must start with us, the youths. This is why this book is dedicated to you. May your hearts and minds be enlightened as you read and take into consideration the principles and ideas discussed herein.

To the millions of youths worldwide, particularly those living in developing nations. May this simple and easy-to-read manual be a source of inspiration and motivation to help you realise that you are worthy and that you were created to shine bright and do amazing things.

It is my prayer and hope that we will reach our full potentials, exercise our responsibilities, and live happy and fulfilled lives.

To my mother, Elizabeth Nyaraye Gatluak, and late father, Daniel Dang, for their unreserved love and care that made me who I am today.

Acknowledgements

Significant accomplishments are by the contributions of many hands and committed spirits. This work is no different. Foremost, I would like to extend my sincere thanks and gratitude to God, who entrusted me with the gift and inspiration to extend His message of peace, hope, and love to the world.

Next, I give special thanks to all my mentors and those who have inspired me, the men I deeply admire. I thank Dr Douglas H. Johnson, an American scholar who lives in Britain who specialises in the history of North East Africa, Sudan and the Southern Sudan for his generous support. I thank Peter Lual Reech Deng, founder & CEO of Africa World Books, for editing and publishing this book. I thank Dr Chuar Juet Jock, Mr John Jock Gatwech, and Mr G. Bang Biel. Without their constructive contribution, this work would not have been possible.

Last but not least, my thanks go to all my relatives, friends, and colleagues, particularly Gabriel Puot Gatbel, Muoch Gach Gatluak, Buay Gatthep Lual, David Yar Ruach, Paul Ruot Juol, Bol Both Majack, William Gatbel Nyoak, Koat Kun Khor, Talimat Nhial Kong, Lim Bol Thong, Philip Pidak Kong, Bichiok Dor Nyith, Gatewech Gatbel Banygaach, Peter Ruach Dak, and Dicheni M.

I acknowledge these peoples' emotional, psychological, and spiritual support, which played a significant role in the process of writing of this book. I can think of no better gift to offer you individually than this book, but only God knows the rewards and blessings He has in store for each one of you.

May this nation and your community be full of peace, love, and unity as you continue to demonstrate positive examples of youth.

To those whose names have not appeared here but who supported, encouraged, and challenged me in one way or another to do and be the best I can be, this work would not have been possible without your tremendous contribution and support. Thank you.

Foreword

Youth is a critical period in a person's life. This stage of life consists of risks and opportunities. When it is spent properly, it can be a blessing to a person and those around them. On the other hand, when this precious time is misused or wasted, it can have catastrophic and dangerous results, not only on an individual level, but on society at large.

This is one of the main reasons why young people are advised and encouraged in this eye-opening book to stand tall, think positively, and behave responsibly as they approach adulthood and late adulthood.

The writer has addressed the most crucial areas of life in which young people should strive to improve themselves, thus making their lives useful and worthy and fostering development into men and women of value in this changing world.

Reading and enacting the ideas and principles presented in this handbook will help you gain the most valuable gifts in life. These are the gifts of knowledge and wisdom, and they are the key drivers to attaining and living a life of faith, purpose, and service, both in this world and in the world to come.

Gatluak D. Thoat,
Peace Worker, Preacher, & Writer

Introduction

The world today is in deep chaos because it is disrupted by the many problems that arise from the social and political mess of our time. These problems include crime, violence, robbery, human trafficking, killing, massacres and genocides, sexual immorality, drug and substance addiction, alcoholism, and more. These human-triggered problems endanger the lives and overall wellbeing of people more often than natural disasters do.

We live in a world where immorality takes the place of morality; killing each other for no reason is common; violence has become the music we sing. We live in a world where peace, forgiveness, love, and unity have become odd and irritating words that some people don't even want to hear about.

The majority, if not all, of these problems are often carried by or through a particular group within our society: young people, who are strong and capable enough to do the job properly.

These young people are, in a sense, confused about their responsibility and position in society. They have lost sight of what it means to be young and of what one ought to do during these precious years of growth and development. They do things with no regard to how their actions might negatively affect them or those around them.

These young people often choose what is wrong over what is right, moral, and socially acceptable. As a result of such a rampant involvement of young people in wrongful acts and crimes, our prisons and streets are filled with precious youths, who should be agents of change, contributing enormously to national development and state-building. This is the saddest and most dangerous part of our changing world.

But in spite of the problems and challenges we are facing today, young people should not be seen as inherently problematic. Instead, they should be viewed as people full of dreams and potential. All they need is the right kind of help and support to enable them to shape their attitudes positively and contribute to our world in significant ways.

This book, *Youths: The Agents of Change & Development*, aims to encourage and challenge young people to become better and more responsible people of purpose, value, and worth.

The first chapter will discuss the importance and power of being a young person. This is important because it is in this precious and energetic period of life that a person can start enacting positive change in his/her own life and those of others.

The second chapter will cover the essence, power, and significance of education, which Mandela said was the only weapon powerful enough to change the world. It takes intellectual and moral education to help a person change him/herself, his/her community or nation, and the entire world. Education enlightens the mind and gives the heart new purpose.

Chapter three will discuss the social responsibility of young people. In this changing world, social responsibility is thought to be exercised only by a particular group within society. This is untrue. As President Franklin D. Roosevelt once said, 'We cannot always build the future for our youth. We can build our youth for the future.' Social responsibility is the duty of everyone, especially young people, to whom the present and future belong. We are not accidents in this world. We are intentional. To make this world a better place, we must carry out our social responsibility as often as possible. Our responsibility is to engage actively in the betterment of ourselves, our families, our communities, our nations, and the world as a whole.

Chapter four will address how you, as a young person, can use education effectively to make an impact on your world. It will discuss the power of young people in engaging in the processes of peacemaking and peace-building, stability, and national and global development.

Chapter five will discuss the enemy, the devil, and his strategies of using pain and the pleasure to render us faithless, hopeless, unproductive, and fruitless. The enemy is against us. He is a deceiver. His primary purpose is to prevent us from recognising, realising, living, and fulfilling our true selves, to obstruct us from achieving our potential. Satan's biggest trap is to keep us busy doing things we are not supposed to do, thus preventing us from knowing and doing the will of our Father in heaven. This is because Satan knows that when young people turn their hearts and minds in faith and obedience to God, he will lose everything.

The sixth chapter will outline what God has said, as revealed to us by His holy words, to and about young people. God has said very clearly what is expected of each one of us while we are in this stage of development. God is our creator. He knows the purpose of each one of us. Knowing and understanding His eternal purpose for our lives is the only way to keep our integrity and character intact. God can pick you up if you come to Him in faith. Whatever problem you may be having right now isn't permanent. God is still in control. He has the power to turn any situation around. All you need to do is have unshakable and unmovable trust and hope in Him and His son, Jesus Christ.

The seventh chapter will discuss the power of living by faith in God. This is the key to becoming who you are. Faith in God is a powerhouse from which you can draw discipline, self-control, positivity, hope, confidence, and other ingredients required for success.

I hope you enjoy this book.

Chapter One

The Importance and Power of Being Young

'Youth is not a time of life; it is a state of mind; it is not a matter of rosy cheeks, red lips, and supple knees; it is a matter of will, a quality of the imagination, a vigour of the emotions; it is the freshness of the deep springs of life.'
                                                                    Samuel Ullman

All living organisms, including human beings, grow and develop, starting at birth and ending with death. For people, this constant transition is marked by various stages of life. There are, of course, several stages of growth and development through which all of us pass. These are the stages of infancy, toddlerhood, adolescence, young adulthood, middle age, and late adulthood.

Ages classified as falling within the youth category vary from place to place, depending on the political, environmental, and socioeconomic situation of a given location. For instance, in some lands, such as the United Kingdom, the United States of America, and some other Western countries, people are generally considered to be youths from the ages of twelve to twenty-five. Conversely, in many parts of the developing world, a person enters youth at the age of fifteen or eighteen and continues to be considered as such until they are 30 or 40 years of age.

Regardless of the effects of political, socioeconomic, and environmental conditions of specific locations on the perceived age of youth, it is generally true that any person above the age of eighteen is permitted by law to vote and to elect and be elected. People over the age of eighteen can, in most places, join military forces and be held responsible and accountable by the law, going through judicial and legal trials and punishments when found guilty of criminal offences. Young people at this age can also be entrusted with specific responsibilities, depending on their educational experiences and qualifications.

One reason for recruiting young people to take part in such social services is that people of this age are considered fit, capable, and healthy enough to do these jobs effectively. Another reason is that people of this age, especially when properly educated and trained, are considered to be mentally, socially, and morally aware of what is right and wrong, good and evil.

Youthful years are among the most beautiful years in one's life. This is a period during which one can bring change and make a difference in the community, nation, and world. When spent responsibly, youth is a period in which a person can achieve success. But when this period of life is misused, the result is disastrous to everyone—family members, friends, neighbours, community members, and fellow citizens.

The wasting of youth is demonstrated by the fact that many young people today are roaming the streets of our towns and cities, robbing people, taking drugs, fighting others, stealing items, committing crimes, and enacting violence. Some of these young people feel hopeless and worthless. This feeling of worthlessness may come as a result of personal problems, family issues, poor upbringings, employment issues, or political instability forcing people to leave their homes and live in crowded places, such as refugee camps and other places where there is scarcity or deficit of social services.

However, despite all challenges, young people can make a positive difference if they remain conscious and alert about the experiences life has brought them. Life is full of ups and downs. Problems and bad situations occur. Today may be bitter and harsh, but tomorrow may be sweeter, especially if you make good use of today, staying strong despite difficult or painful situations.

Pain is often seen in the stories of successful people. Some of these stories include risk of personal harm. In contrast, others include problems facing entire populations, like those South Sudan and many other war-torn nations have endured over recent years. Pain and bad situations are normal parts of life. They are inevitable and unpredictable, but they teach us to understand life better. Our experiences enable us to shape our attitudes positively, maturing and learning to resist what we can endure, stay mentally healthy in the face of adversity, and accept problems and circumstances that we cannot change.

Young people are the building blocks of every strong nation. This is because they are at the stage of growth and development where they are physically, mentally, and spiritually able to contribute in compelling and meaningful ways, especially when they are well taught and prepared to handle such responsibilities. Young people are full of energy and enthusiasm about what they want to achieve. They are active and excited about being valued and respected in their society.

Youth, once it is wasted, doesn't come back. For this reason, all of us who are in this critical stage should be alert, diligent, and committed to using this it in ways that benefit ourselves, our families, our neighbours, our communities, and our nation as a whole. Youthful years should be lived with care and determination. Youth is a period of benefits and risks.

Youth is a Time of Personal Organisation and Preparation

Preparation for the success of tomorrow begins in youth. Youth is a period of transition in which we prepare ourselves ready for what we want to do or become later in life. It is a period of mental, emotional, and spiritual preparation for lifelong success. This is why schooling takes place during the early years of life. As one writer says, the success of tomorrow begins today. Youth is the right time to prepare yourself to become somebody in the future. It should not be taken for granted.

Youth is a Period of Hard Work and Commitment

In youth, individuals must work hard to achieve their visions, giving them purpose in life. Anything worthy takes energy and time. Thus, hard work has no substitute when it comes to attaining success. For example, before I could write this book, I had to be a good reader. I read a lot. This enabled me to learn and generate ideas and thoughts worth writing. It takes hard work and commitment to achieve what you want to do, and this must start now, in your youth.

Youth is a Period to Start Influencing, Inspiring, and Making a Difference

We are all here for a reason. No one is an accident. Sadly, only a small number of people realise this while they are still young. God created each one of us with all that we need to make a difference in the world. We are born with the potential to do anything.

All the amazing things we see around us are the results of the hard work and commitment of our brothers and sisters, who decided to improve lives and make this world a better place. You too can achieve your dreams, especially when you consult God, your creator, to give you insights and revelations about what you should do to help and shape your generation and those that follow. The earlier you realise your purpose, the sweeter and more fulfilling your life will be. Money and material wealth cannot make life comfortable and fulfilling, but serving your gift can.

We all know what Mandela went through during his fight for a free and united South Africa. He was sent to prison, where he remained for twenty-seven years. Mandela would have died in prison or shortly after he was released if he had not been so young and strong when he was jailed. He would not have gone on to serve as president. Two things kept him physically and mentally steady: his youthfulness and his purpose—his passion and conviction to fight against injustice and inequality. Youth is the period in which you can influence and inspire others and make a difference using your physical and mental strengths.

Youth is a Period in which to Create a Positive Legacy

A legacy is what you hand down to people or generations after you and your own. There are only two things for which a person can be remembered after death: good deeds and evil deeds. We should all work to do good deeds. Once a person does what they are supposed to do, a positive legacy for future generations is created.

A good legacy has to do with the hearts you have touched and the lives you have changed or influenced in your life. Youth is a period in which to do good things that will outlive you. It is a period in which you should spend your energy and zeal to make sure that the next generation is proud of how you lived. This way, your legacy will be a source of inspiration, motivation, and courage for others. As one minister said, our greater and deeper fear should not be death but living without doing anything that would make the next generation proud of us.

Youths should strive to live responsibly. We are created with all the ingredients needed for success. Everything we need to make it through life is inside every one of us. Once you discover your purpose in life and follow that vision with faith and determined effort, you will begin to construct a legacy that will change and reshape the world. The right time to start acting and living the life of your dreams is now, in youth.

CHAPTER TWO:

Youth and Education

The foundation of every state is the education of its youth.'

Diogenes

The word 'education' comes from the Latin word *'educere'* meaning 'to lead out.'[1] Education can be defined as the relentless process of becoming. According to Wikipedia, education, in its broadest sense, is any act or experience that has a formative effect on the mind, character, or physical ability of an individual. In its technical sense, education is a process by which people deliberately share accumulated knowledge, skills, and values. These two definitions are essential in informing our understanding of what education is. They demonstrate the intellectual and moral value and meaning of education.

The Purpose of Education

Youth is the phase of life in which people dream big and hope for the best, looking towards a bright tomorrow. It is a phase of life in

---

1 Education—Meaning, Origin, History and Philosophy

which nothing seems impossible. In this period, people often want to be successful, and they believe that success is possible. During these years, life looks bright and beautiful.

Transitioning from a being child or a teenager to an adult is a big step, marking growth towards a new phase of life. Several qualities are required to help you live as a moral and righteous person. There is a need to add discipline, self-control, confidence, and responsibility to your life. Youth is the phase of life in which you begin to understand yourself, discover your potential, and recognise opportunities for success. It is a time to reinvent yourself and design your personality. Education has an important role to play in this process.

Education is the backbone of every successful society. It is the foundation upon which the growth of society is built. Education is the basis for the development and empowerment of every nation. It plays a vital role in helping people understand and participate in the activities of today's world. It builds character and is significant in transmitting cultures, beliefs, and values. Education is essential for fostering innovation and meeting the needs of a nation.

The development of a nation is not measured by the buildings it has built, the roads it has laid down, or the bridges it has constructed. It is measured by human resources and the capacity of citizens to maintain such constructions. Education is crucial not only to equip new generations with skills to earn livelihoods but also to create awareness of social and environmental realities and to encourage the independence of mind and spirit that are paramount to the moulding of responsible citizens.

Generally speaking, the importance of education does not require any emphasis. The fundamental purpose of education is to transfigure and transform the human personality into a pattern of perfection through the synthetic processes of the development of the body, the enrichment and enlightenment of the mind, and the illumination of the spirit. The growth of society is not possible without education. It is for this reason that almost all eminent educationists unanimously agree that education is the pillar upon which nations rest.

Young people's education is incredibly important, and nations should take it seriously. The future of every country is built on its young and upcoming generations. Training of young people should not only focus on intellect but also on morality.

Youth education is the most solid foundation for the success of a nation. Governments come and go, the land and its people remain. When young generations are properly educated, lives can be improved.

Education is robust because it helps the mind and spirit to work together. It enlightens the mind to think innovatively and creatively. Through the process of learning, we learn and develop the ingredients for success.

Education is a Path Leader for Young People

Youth is a phase of significant change. During this stage, young people become mature and responsible adults. Education helps young people to choose and seek positive directions in life. Through education, young people can set goals for themselves and strive to achieve them. Education propels youth in the right direction. It is a path leader.

Education Makes Young People Self-Aware

As someone who was displaced by the violent conflict that erupted in December 2013 in my country, I stayed in one of the refugee camps in Gambella, Ethiopia, for over a year before I could attend college to study. A lot of things happened as I watched and observed the lives of my people. Problems such as overcrowding, inter-communal violence, teen and unplanned pregnancy, unplanned marriage, sexually transmitted diseases (STDs), and self-induced abortion were faced by many young people.

But these problems are not only seen or heard of in places like refugee camps. They are growing concerns in every land in our modern world. These issues have become increasingly widespread as a result of a lack of sex education programs.

Incomplete or partial knowledge about sex can lead young people to engage in dangerous sexual activities. Education makes young people self-aware. It imparts knowledge and skills that can be used to protect young people from harmful or unwanted challenges.

Education Makes Young People Socially Aware

Education can help young people develop an awareness of current social, economic, and environmental issues. Knowledge also helps young people contribute to solving those issues.

Education exposes youths to the darker side of society, the problems that eclipse it, the prejudices that shackle it, and the superstitions that blind it. Therefore, education encourages youths to come up with ideas to better the society of which they are part.

Education Brings Financial Stability

Poverty knocks at almost every door in developing countries. A proper education enables youths to find excellent and well-paid jobs that help them stabilise their finances. Education is required not only to find work but also to help individuals track and monitor incomes and budgets effectively. Extravagancy is a growing problem affecting a number of people, and it depletes income quickly, but financial education can help to reduce this problem. School teaches us how to live as well as how to make a living.

Education Aids Development of Leadership Skills

Leadership can be learned. When youths are provided with proper education, they can learn to be effective leaders. The need for high-quality education for young leaders is now more profound than ever. The world is becoming an increasingly dangerous place to live because of political leadership problems. When youths are intellectually and morally educated, they can look beyond borders, and their attitudes can change. They can develop positive attitudes and self-esteem. Education can also develop and broaden interpersonal skills. Young people can learn how to shoulder leadership responsibilities and powers in the most effective and honest ways possible.

The Power of Education

Education is the key to personal, communal, and societal development. Genuine maturity is about much more than physical maturity. Real maturity involves and encompasses physical, social, mental, emotional, and spiritual maturity. Proper education is desperately needed for young people. Why? Because education does not just give you wings. It also strengthens them, enabling you to fly higher in life. Consider the story below.

> *Many years ago, a farmer found a baby eagle in a bush. He took it home, placed it among his chickens, and fed it chicken food. Very soon, the baby eagle forgot that it was an eagle, the king of the birds. It ate chicken food and did as chickens do. It was just like a chicken.*
>
> *One very good day, a traveller came to the farm where the birds were kept. When he looked at the birds playing and eating, he said to the farmer, "That bird is an eagle, isn't it?"*

"No," the farmer replied. "It was an eagle, but now it is a chicken. It looks down to the ground and eats chicken food."

The traveller asked, "May I take the eagle and try to teach it to be an eagle again?"

"You may try," said the farmer. "But you won't be able to do anything. It looks to the ground and eats chicken food. It has forgotten that it was ever an eagle."

The traveller took the eagle. He held it up and said, "Eagle, you are an eagle. Look up. Your place is near the sun. Stretch your wings and fly."

But the eagle would not look up. It looked down and saw the chicken food, and it jumped to the ground and began to eat.

The traveller tried again and again. Each day, the traveller held up the eagle's head and said, "Lookup. You are an eagle. Stretch out your wings, and fly up to the sun." But each time, the eagle soon looked to the ground and jumped down and ate chicken food.

The traveller went on and on trying, and at last, one beautiful day, the eagle threw back its head and looked up at the sun. It remembered that it was an eagle. It stretched its wings and flew straight up and up away to its own place near the sun, and it never came back to look at the ground and eat chicken food again.[2]

What are the morals of this story?
- We were made for great things, but we must believe in ourselves. We are eagles. We must stretch our mental, emotional, and spiritual wings and fly up not only to the sun but to our final

---

2   Adapted from *The Oxford English Reader for Africa*, book 3, 2nd edition, p.120.

destination: heaven.
- We must educate our minds, hearts, and spirits, enabling us to stretch our wings and fly higher.
- We must strive to work as hard and as best as we can, to be as good as we can be, and to make the world as safe and peaceful as it should be.

Education is the best tool to bring positive change to society and contribute to the development of good human beings. The fundamental purpose of education is to share knowledge. Education is powerful. It is an instrument for the realisation of one's innate self and one's strengths. It is essential. Thus, those who do not have access to education may be prone to choosing the wrong paths in life. Through education, we know where we came from. The Bible educates us about God, who created us from nothing.

True Education

Who do we call educated? Socrates said the following:

> *'First, those who manage well the circumstances which they encounter day by day; and those who can judge situations appropriately as they arise and rarely miss the suitable course of action.*
>
> *Next, those who are honorable in their dealings with all men, bearing easily what is unpleasant or offensive in others and being as reasonable with their associates as is humanly possible. Furthermore, those who hold their pleasures always under control and are not unduly overcome by their misfortunes, bearing up under them bravely and in a manner worthy of our universal nature.*

> *Most important of all, those who are not spoiled by their successes, who do not desert their true selves, but hold their ground steadfastly as wise and sober-minded men, rejoicing no more in the good things that have come to them through chance than in those which through their own nature and intelligence are theirs since birth.*
>
> *Those who have a character which is in accord, not with one of these things, but with all of them, these are educated — possessed of all the virtues.'*
>
> Socrates (469-399 BCE)

As we conclude this chapter, I remind you that education is powerful and vital to personal, social, and professional life. Education is a factor of change in the lives of individuals and in society as a whole. Education is a tool that young people can and should use to equip themselves as valuable members of the community and to realise their potential. Youths should be provided with the best possible education and given favourable conditions to support the attainment of skills and wisdom.

Every nation, especially developing countries, should strive to give young people opportunities to contribute to society while fulfilling their potential. Nations should work to provide adequate and sound education systems that can help young people discover and unleash their potentials, therefore learning to live responsibly as agents and assets of change.

> *'Literacy is a bridge from misery to hope. It is a tool for daily life in modern society. It is a bulwark against poverty, and a building block of development, an essential complement to investments in roads, dams, clinics, and factories. Literacy is a platform for democ-*

ratisation, and a vehicle for the promotion of cultural and national identity. Especially for girls and women, it is an agent of family health and nutrition. For everyone, everywhere, literacy is, along with education in general, a basic human right ... Literacy is, finally, the road to human progress and the means through which every man, woman, and child can realise his or her full potential.'

Kofi Annan

CHAPTER THREE

Youth and Social Responsibility

*'Our prime purpose in life is to help others.
And if you can't help them, at least don't hurt them.'*
Dalai Lama

We come to this earth with a clear purpose. We are all created by God to stay connected with Him and to do all things for His glory. God is righteous. He is just and moral. It is with this concept of the morality that we will discuss our responsibility to our communities, our families, and ourselves.

There is only one planet suitable for living organisms to live and reproduce on. Earth is the only place God has provided for us, and He has placed His creations here to enjoy the wonderful gift of life. Human beings are, however, also placed here to carry out the critical responsibility of making this planet a better and more suitable environment for all the other humans who share it. We are required to make good use of this planet. We are required to take as good care of it as possible.

This means that each one of us has a role in shaping and caring for this world. This responsibility should start with our communities, families, and selves. We should put the wellbeing of our family, community, and nation before our own. This is social responsibility. Unfortunately, our society is degenerating because many have turned their backs on this responsibility, putting personal gain before the needs of others.

People do not care for others anymore. Social and moral obligations such as respect for elders, charity for the poor, and support for social and community activities are far from the minds of many young people today. These social and moral obligations are increasingly being replaced by juvenile delinquency, crime, disrespect for elders, theft, and so on.

Several factors make young people misbehave or resort to antisocial behaviours. Unemployment, family problems, and peer pressures and are some of the factors that steer young people away from their moral obligations. We must bear in mind that the presence of such factors doesn't justify running away from responsibilities or misbehaving. We are expected to meet our social and moral obligations as always, despite the presence of pressuring circumstances in our changing world.

'When we meet real tragedy in life, we can react in two ways—either by losing hope and falling into self-destructive habits, or by using the challenge to find our inner strength.'

Dalai Lama

Problems inevitably occur, coming from different sources. Sometimes, unpredictable circumstances are created by political leaders, who use us—young people—to fight for their own interests and ambitions. Other times, problems arise as a result of our actions as we turn to the streets to satisfy our needs at the expense of other people. Taking shortcuts or using illegitimate means to satisfy our wants and needs is wrong and can lead to adverse outcomes. What goes around, comes around. When we do bad things to get what we want, bad will come back and find us.

Faith and patience are essential qualities to possess when things do not work out the way we want them to. We all possess the potential to make it through life. The bad breaks of life that come to our way do not have to lead us down the wrong paths. Our task as youths is to stay vigilant, self-controlled, and active enough to avoid trying to satisfy our desires and interests in the wrong ways, even if making the right choices means losing something special. We must stay faithful and patient when the darkest parts of life hit us. We all have the potential to make the best of life. The presence of a temporary setback prepares us for the next opportunity.

> *'When you are at the top, be careful of the monster called PRIDE. Pride will make you look down on the people who haven't attained your level of success.*
>
> *When you are at the bottom, be careful of the monster called BITTERNESS. Bitterness will make you jealous and think that other people are the reason you haven't made it.*
>
> *When you are on the way to the top, be careful of the monster called GREED. Greed will make you impatient and make you steal or seek shortcuts.*
>
> *When you are on your way down, be careful of the monster called DESPAIR. Despair will make you think it's all over, yet there is still hope.'*
>
> Nelson Mandela

Responsibility and freedom go hand in hand. Every good citizen should shoulder their share of responsibility to better their community. The betterment of our lives and the lives of those around us depends on the compassion, goodness, and kindness that we all contribute to society.

How to Be a Good Person

Being a good person does not come from inactivity or keeping silent as you watch bad things happen. Refraining from stealing, cheating, and lying is not enough to make you a good person. Being a good person comes from doing good things, not merely from refraining from doing bad things.

Remaining silent in the face of injustice and inequality prevents you from being the right person. Why? Because by staying silent, you demonstrate a lack of empathy and compassion, refusing to stand up and care for others. Contributing fairness, courage, compassion, loyalty, sympathy, courtesy, integrity, and humility to your community is what makes you the right person. Those who learn such values always stand up for justice. They give help to those in need. They are dependable. They make life better for themselves and those around them.

Social responsibility means contributing your worth to your community. It means living in such a way that safeguards the wellbeing of those around you.

Do Good to Be Remembered as Good

Responsible citizens should always strive to do and offer their best to the people around them. They should do this not to gain popularity or to earn praise but because it is part of their responsibility as citizens.

When we do good freely for people who can't pay us back, we can achieve great satisfaction in life. But how can we do good for others who can't pay us in return? Well, as a citizen, there are several ways you can support the wellbeing of your community and nation. All you need to do is be willing to help in whatever way you can.

Identify the Type of Citizen You Are Now and the Type You Will Be in the Future[3]

A study of democratic citizenship suggested that citizens can be categorised into three different types of citizenship based on their civic participation. These are as follows:

Personally Responsible Citizens

Personally responsible citizens are citizens who:
- act responsibly in their community
- work and pay taxes
- obey the law of the land
- recycle and donate food
- volunteer to help others in times of crisis.

Sample Action:
- Contribute to a food drive to help others.

Core Assumption/Belief:
- To solve social problems and improve society, citizens must have good character. They must be honest, responsible, and law-abiding members of the community.

Personally responsible citizens are individuals who are generous, humble, and kind towards other people, regardless of race, gender, ethnicity, political and socio-economic background, and so on.

---

3   Adapted from Civic Education workshop for young people in Timor Leste, participants' notebook, p.22

'Generosity and kindness will be rewarded: give a cup of water, and you will receive a cup of water in return.'
Proverbs 11:25 CEV

Participatory Citizens

Participatory citizens are citizens who:
- are active members of community, organisation, and/or improvement efforts
- organise community efforts to care for those in need and promote economic development
- know how government agencies work
- know strategies for accomplishing collective tasks.

Sample Action:
- Help to organise a food drive that can be contributed to by personally responsible citizens.

Core Assumption/Belief:
- To solve social problems and improve society, citizens must actively participate and take leadership position(s) within established political and community structures or systems.

In a nutshell, participatory citizens are citizens who are loving and empathetic. They see the needs of others and act with love and compassion to offer solutions.

'Let love and loyalty always show like a necklace, and write them in your mind. God and people will like you and consider you a success.'
Proverbs 3:3-6 CEV

Justice-Oriented Citizens

Justice-oriented citizens are citizens who:
- critically assess social, political, and economic structures to see beyond the surface
- address areas of injustice
- know about social movements and how to affect systemic change.

Sample Action:
- Ask why people are hungry, and act to solve the root cause(s) of the problem.

Core Assumption/Belief:
- To solve social problems and improve society, citizens must question and change established systems and structures that produce patterns of injustice.

> *'When justice is done, good citizens are glad and crooks are terrified.'*
>
> Proverbs 21:15 CEV

To summarise, personally responsible citizens demonstrate and act on traits of honesty, responsibility, integrity, and respect for the law. Participatory citizens see themselves as possessing good character traits, understand government structures, vote in elections, and volunteer in community services. Justice-oriented citizens fight for the rights of the underprivileged and are often willing to suffer personal harm in their fight for injustice. If participatory citizens organise a food drive and personally responsible citizens donate food, justice-oriented citizens ask why people are hungry and act upon the root cause of suffering.

What type of citizen are you? Or what type of citizen do you want to be? What are you doing right now to achieve this goal? National development and state-building are the responsibilities of everyone. You can contribute to this collective process by acting responsibly as an honest, compassionate, fair, and just citizen, doing your share for your community.

The people around you do not only need material help from you. Perhaps more importantly, they need your love and respect. They need to be treated with dignity and decency. They need to be valued, not devalued. That is why you should always be responsible for your words and actions.

CHAPTER FOUR

YOUTH AND PEACE AND SECURITY

'Young people should be at the forefront of global change and innovation. Empowered, they can be key agents for development and peace. If, however, they are left on society's margin, all of us will be impoverished. Let us ensure that all young people have every opportunity to participate fully in the lives of their societies.'

Kofi Annan

The modern world is becoming smaller, transforming into a global village that is highly integrated and technologically advanced. However, it is also becoming more fragmented and unsafe and less peaceful for current and future generations. If no proper conflict resolution measures are established collectively to maintain peace and security, this will continue to worsen. The world is increasingly plagued by tension, violence, declining values, and less respect for human rights.

Youths are often victims of violence and conflict, and they are also often the perpetrators of such violence and conflict. The culture of guns and abuse has become a significant concern in most developing countries, threatening the futures of young people, who deserve a peaceful life.

Young people are targeted and recruited to join terrorism and violence-oriented groups; young people are gathered and armed by politicians to target groups of people that are identified as enemies. Young people are often used as tools, carrying out orders and commands, and little to no regard is given to whether or not such orders and commands will negatively impact on them or society.

Youths are the pillars that keep their nations upright. This means that the quality of a nation's peace and security is determined by whether its youths are valued and given opportunities to participate fully in issues concerning the wellbeing of their people. Youths are frontline agents of change. Thus, their input and inclusion in developmental programs can go a long way towards achieving objectives.

How Youths Can Be the Change, They Want to Be

Young people are agents of change in local, regional, and global contexts. One reason for this is because youth is a period of enthusiasm, passion, vigour, ambition, and hope. These virtues can enable youths to play a significant role in peace and conflict resolution mechanisms.

Youths can enact change by being able to change themselves. This is mandatory. No one can have an impact on society unless they first have had an effect on themselves. Young people wishing to contribute towards shaping society must change the attitude towards people, traditions, religions, and beliefs.

By realising their purpose and meaning in life, young people can create a haven both for themselves and for others. Sadly, though, youths living in some of the world's most conflict-affected countries find it difficult to acknowledge their worth and value. They live in emotional prisons of guilt, worthlessness, and hopelessness.

Many youths from areas affected by conflict and violence are highly traumatised, sometimes to the point of suicidality. Negative thoughts and emotions cloud their reasoning, and they resort to drugs and alcohol to calm psychological battles with resentment, anxiety, fear, guilt, and depression. This makes precious and promising youths more prone to engaging in violence and other illicit activities.

Despite all of this, youths can still create the change they want to see because they carry within themselves the capacity to change and live as they desire.

Accept and Resolve the Frictions of Life

Life has its ups and downs. There are some situations and circumstances that are beyond our understanding and control. Sometimes, unthinkable things happen against our wishes and expectations. Often, such things help us learn and develop life experience. This is liberating. Our destiny is not determined by what happens to us; it is determined by what we do about what happens.

When we are faced with challenges, we must remember that we possess the capacity to resolve the emotional and psychological frictions that try to dictate our thoughts and actions. This process has to do with channelling ideas and transforming attitudes in spite of what life throws our way.

> *'The greatest discovery of my generation is that human beings can alter their lives by altering their attitudes of mind.'*
>
> William James

Peace and Development Go Hand in Hand

We cannot separate peace and development. The absence of the former prevents the latter. Youths are great resources in every nation. When young people are actively involved in developmental programs, goals can be achieved. This is one of the reasons why when things go wrong, the solution is to educate young people on how to fix them and let go of the past, moving forward and into the future.

Youths can take part in creating a peaceful and stable environments actively. However, for these things to work as desired, youths need the support of those currently in positions of leadership, who should realise that young people can create positive change when involved in political processes and national development.

Youths should not be regarded as threats. Our society needs to look beyond the surface. All over the world, young people are struggling to find their positions in social and political spheres. They are eager to make their voices heard, to offer ideas for consideration, and to participate fully in the affairs of their countries.

For instance, in South Sudan, a country crippled by war for many years, people, particularly youths, have become hopeless, but things can still change for the better. It is possible for people to live comfortably. When we, as youths, change, circumstances can and will change also. The stability of our countries rests on our shoulders. We must change ourselves so as to bring the desired positive change and stability to our nations.

As young people, we can change ourselves by forgiving one another. We have been fighting each other for too many years. It's up to us now to redirect our thoughts and actions towards creating a better communal life for our generation and for those to come. It is our task and responsibility to allow the emotional wounds and bitterness of our past to heal. We can do this by letting go of grudges and focusing on love, compassion, and unity.

An Eye for an Eye Makes the Whole World Blind

Several factors disrupt peace and security. One of these is revenge. According to Wikipedia, revenge is defined as the act of inflicting harm upon a person or group in response to a grievance, be it perceived or real. Revenge is an unlawful means of punishment.

Revenge killing is a rampant and growing issue endangering peace and security in many parts of the world, including South Sudan. Revenge acts have been occurring for centuries. But God, who knows everything, warns us not to seek revenge. God tells us to forgive. He wants us to live safely and in harmony with each other. We, as human beings, do not have the ability to bring back what is already gone, so by exacting revenge, we can only risk our future.

Unfortunately, some traditional cultures and beliefs make it difficult for their observers to comprehend this idea of refraining from revenge or retaliation. Some of these cultures deem being merciful and forgiving cowardly. In these cultures, failure or refusal to take revenge is often regarded as unmanly. This encourages the cycle of revenge to repeat itself, as most young men do not want to be considered as cowardly or unmanly. They strive to prove their manhood and strength by taking revenge.

Social Psychologist Ian McKee stated that 'people who are more vengeful tend to be those who are motivated by power, by authority, and by the desire for status. They don't want to lose face.'[4]

Writer Michael Ignatief put it this way:

'Revenge is a profound moral desire to keep faith with the dead, to honour their memory by taking up their cause where they left off.'[5]

---

4   , https//www.en.m.wikipedia.org/wiki/Revenge, accessed on April 4, 2019

5   http//www.en.m.wikipedia.org/wiki/Revenge, accessed on April 4, 2019

Honour passes from generation to generation, inciting instances of revenge and retaliation. Myths and perceived negative information surround the practice of forgiveness and reconciliation among people. However, God, through the Bible, tells us that we should refrain from taking revenge.

God loves us all. His love is far greater than the love we have for our loved ones, who might have fallen victim to the revenge acts of another person or group. It is important that we leave things up to God and do not risk our lives, or those of others, for the sake of revenge.

Revenge is bitter and deadly. It creates misery in this life and in the life to come. Often, the relatives of victims of revenge killings hunt or kill perpetrators, further perpetuating the revenge cycle. And those who do not repent for the sin of murder will answer to God on judgement day.

'He who seeks revenge digs two graves.'
Chinese proverb

As youths, we can change ourselves by refusing to be used as tools against our countrymen and women. We must resist, at all costs, to put the lives of innocent men, women, and children in danger. We should not be the vehicles for another person's hatred and bitterness. We have great things to do, and we should not waste our precious time on things that bring no good. There is no need to die for reasons that are not worth fighting for.

We can generate the change we deserve by not allowing anybody to divide us through political or ethnic incitement. We are tired of wars and violent conflicts. We deserve to live in peace.

Accepting prejudices that outline specific people or groups as enemies is the worst thing we can do. It is poison that can harm and kill. Youths can create the change they want to see by standing up for justice and equality. Unfortunately, some youths have lost sight of this. They are passive and often timid when they see injustice and inequality. They remain silent, especially when those responsible for acts of injustice are from their ethnic group or share a political ideology with them. Remember, you are a citizen who shares the same human and democratic rights as everyone around you, regardless of your differences.

'If you are neutral in situation of injustice, you have chosen the side of the oppressor.'
Bishop Desmond Tutu

What good is it to remain silent while your friends, colleagues, and fellow citizens are targeted and pushed out of the system because they do not conform to dominant ethnic or political backgrounds? Stand against injustice and inequality whenever they appear, even if that could mean losing your position or status. These things are temporary, but integrity is eternal, and this is what defines you as a responsible human being.

This doesn't mean that you should take arms and create violence whenever or wherever you see injustice and inequality being exercised. What it means is that a non-violent approach to situations of injustice can be incredibly powerful. Your voice matters.

Young people can bring lasting peace and security to the nation by choosing to refrain from violence when confronted with conflict. Violence is not the solution to disputes and misunderstandings. Violence does not solve problems. It only worsens and darkens them. Peaceful resolution is always the best option.

'Returning hate for hate multiplies hate, adding deeper darkness to a night already devoid of stars. Darkness

cannot drive out darkness; only light can do that. Hate cannot drive out hate; only love can do that.'

Martin Luther King Jr

Young people should have the courage to solve pressing problems. They should always strive to use peaceful means to solve problems, keeping their emotions and tempers under control and not allowing them to dictate their logic, reasoning, or judgement. Your ability to control your emotions and temper, regardless of the intensity of the problem you are faced with, defines your maturity and social responsibility.

What do Youths Expect from their Government(s)?

Young people are the most important and valuable human resources. All governments have a responsibility to protect their people. This protection can be enacted in a number of ways. Governments protect citizens by building correction facilities, training and equipping military and police personnel, making and enforcing laws, appointing honest officials to implement those laws, strengthening civil servants, and so on.

Governments are also responsible for provision. Governments act as providers of goods and services that individuals cannot provide for themselves. They must provide for the needs of their people in a way that is inclusive, equal, and non-discriminatory. Basic infrastructure of human connectivity falls into this category. For example, means of physical travel, such as roads, airports, and bridges, are provided by governments to benefit citizens. Similarly, governments provide education and healthcare, working to enhance and develop the lives of their citizens, especially young people.

Government protection and provision are essential; the overall success of a government building upon these foundations.

Governments must protect citizens from violence and hardship whenever possible. They should strive to provide public goods and services at the level necessary to ensure a globally competitive economy and well-functioning society.

Most importantly, governments should invest in citizens' capabilities, working to enable them to provide for themselves in rapidly changing circumstances.

This brings us to the concept of governments as investors. Young people are full of energy and potential. They need their governments to invest in them. Investing in young people is one of the crucial steps that an active and citizen-centred government should take to ensure a safe, stable, and peaceful society.

> *'The future belongs to our youth. As some of us near the end of our political careers, younger people must take over. They must seek and cherish the most basic condition for peace, namely unity in our diversity, and find lasting ways to that goal.'*
>
> Nelson R. Mandela

Former US president Abraham Lincoln had a similar idea about the responsibilities of government, stating that the mission of a strong government is to stand for the wellbeing of its citizens. By giving citizens, especially young citizens, opportunities and exposing them to new challenges, governments can help their people to develop and realise their true potential.

> *'... government of the people, by the people, for the people, shall not perish from the earth.'*
>
> Abraham Lincoln

CHAPTER FIVE

WATCH OUT! THE DEVIL IS AFTER YOU

'Be alert and of sober mind. Your enemy the devil prowls around like a roaring lion looking for someone to devour.'
1 Peter 5:8 (NIV)

Human beings, particularly young people, are easily manipulated by the devil. It is important for us to talk about this and to notice that which stands against our efforts to succeed in life.

Youth is a period of opportunity, but it is also a period of risks and problems. When this crucial period in one's life is used wisely, the result can be a great sense of fulfilment. When it is misused, the result can be disastrous, both to youths themselves and to society as a whole.

Young people must know and understand that they have an enemy whose primary purpose is to prevent them from achieving what they were born to achieve. This enemy is always working to detach, separate, and distract us from following the right paths, wanting to separate us from the source of life and hope: God.

This enemy is not your neighbour living next door. He is not your family member who refuses to have anything to do with you. He is not your friend who broke your heart years ago. He is not the community member who keeps gossiping about you, nor a member of the clan or tribe/ethnic group who looted your property burned down your shelter or harmed or killed your loved ones. We often consider our enemies to be those who hurt or do us wrong, but this isn't true. The enemy is not a person; it is an evil spirit that uses those individuals against us. He is the devil, the deceiver, and the adversary.

We read from scripture that Satan comes to steal and kill. He is always accusing us of wrongdoings before God. He aims to create our downfall, keeping us from the goodness and glory of God. Satan doesn't want us to succeed with the right things in life. He wants us to succeed in the wrong things, like killing, drinking, smoking, lying, cheating, deceiving, and committing crimes. He wants us to fall short from the saving grace of our merciful Lord.

Satan works day and night to destroy dreams. No one is born without a purpose in life, but Satan fights to prevent people from discovering their purpose. For this reason, it is vital to know and understand his deceptive and discouraging strategies. Only then can we restore lost dreams and work faithfully and victoriously to achieve our God-given purpose.

I faithfully and hopefully believe that after you have read this chapter, you will be able to regain the emotional, psychological, and spiritual energy needed to face life and all of its circumstances with confidence and hope. You will be able to stop bad behaviours and return to wholeheartedly serving God, the creator.

To discuss some of the devil's major deceptive strategies, we must first consider the following questions.

- Have you ever experienced thoughts or feelings that tell you that you won't make it?
- Do you hold a mental picture of what you are going to do or who you're going to be in the future but sometimes feel discouraged, wanting to quit before you get there?

- Do circumstances ever make you think that life is meaningless or that there is no reason to live anymore?
- Do you sometimes view some people as the reason for your failures?
- Do you sometimes feel that it is a burden to be a Christian?
- Do you sometimes think or feel that life is good and enjoyable even without God?

These are just some of the questions and doubts that Satan will throw your way. His tactic is to set you against yourself, encouraging you to hate yourself and others and promoting selfish and self-destructive behaviour.

There are two powerful strategies that the devil uses to control many of us. These are pain and pleasure. He uses these tactics to steer us away from becoming who we are and are made to be. Let's discuss these strategies in further detail.

The Use of Pain and Bad Circumstances

Life is full of unpredictable circumstances. Many things make us cry, mourn, and grieve every single day. These circumstances cause us physical and emotional pain. We feel pain when we encounter death or severe health conditions in ourselves or those we love.

Unfortunately, our response to such painful situations is sometimes more painful and destructive than the conditions themselves. This is why it's imperative to understand the source of pain and suffering. Satan is responsible for almost all the unfortunate and painful circumstances and experiences we encounter in life. When we know this, we can live happy lives of faith and hope.

Satan knows that we humans are weak and vulnerable to what hurts us, physically, emotionally, or both. He may use illness, disaster, poverty, fear, doubt, and even death to discourage us. Why? Because Satan knows that you were created for a purpose, and he does not want you to realise this purpose. Unfortunately, some people are reluctant to accept the fact that the devil intends to keep them under the darkness of self-doubt, fear, anxiety, and depression.

Satan is referred to as the prince of darkness. He aims to discourage us, using painful and hard-to-bear situations. Such things frighten us as human beings, but there is someone mighty enough to help us endure such difficulties.

The Prescription for Pain

Pain, in all of its forms, has an effective cure. Whatever you may be passing through right now, there is a solution to every problem you are facing. This solution is to have faith and hope in Jesus Christ. God created human beings in His image, we need God in our lives to function well and enjoy the gift of life.

What Does Pain Teach Us?

Pain comes from a variety of sources. It may occur as a result of the carelessness that comes with sinful and corrupted attitudes. Regardless of where or who pain comes from, we all carry with us the capacity to turn any painful story into a victory. Consider the short story below.

> *Once upon a time, a daughter complained to her mother that her life was miserable and that she didn't know how she was going to make it. She was tired of fighting and struggling all the time. It seemed that just as one problem was solved, another soon followed. Her mother took her to the kitchen. She filled three pots with water and placed each on a high fire.*

Once the three pots began to boil, she placed potatoes in one pot, eggs in the second pot, and some ground coffee beans in the third pot. She let them sit and boil, not saying a word to her daughter.

The daughter waited impatiently, wondering what her mother was doing.

After twenty minutes, her mother turned the burners off. She took the potatoes out of the pot and placed them in a bowl. She pulled the eggs out and placed them in a bowl. She ladled out the ground coffee beans and placed them in a cup. Turning to her daughter, the mother asked, "Daughter, what do you see?"

"Potatoes, eggs, and ground coffee beans," the daughter replied.

"Come closer," the mother said. "Touch the potatoes."

The daughter did, and she noticed that they were soft.

The mother then asked her to take the egg and break it.

The daughter pulled off the shell and observed the hard-boiled egg.

Finally, the mother asked her daughter to sip the ground coffee beans.

Their rich aroma brought a smile to the daughter's face. "Mother, what is the meaning of all this?" she asked.

Her mother explained that the potatoes, the eggs, and the ground coffee beans had each faced the same adversity — the boiling water. But each one had reacted differently. The potatoes went in strong and hard, but in the boiling water, they became soft and weak. The egg was fragile, its thin outer shell protecting its delicate interior, but in the boiling water, the inside of the egg became hard. And the ground coffee beans were unique. When exposed to the boiling water, they changed the water and created something new.

"Now, which one are you?" the mother asked her daughter. "When adversity knocks on your door, how do you respond? Are you a potato, an egg, or a coffee bean?"

What Can We Learn From This Story?

- In life, things will happen to you and around you, but you have the power to choose how to react to them. You can decide what you will gain from the struggles you face.
- It is important to remember that times of adversity and pain are also times of learning and mental, emotional, and spiritual growth.
- When adversity or pain knocks, be like an egg. Become stronger inside. Tighten your mental, emotional, and spiritual belt, and develop the strength you need to move through the storm of pain.
- Life is all about learning, adapting, and converting hardship into something positive and meaningful. This is possible when you have a stable and unmovable faith and hope in God.

'Turn your wounds into wisdom.'

Oprah Winfrey

Remember, you are judged and defined by what you endure, not by what you escape. Through the storms, hardships, and struggles of life, your character is shaped. You may suffer the emotional and psychological hardships of divorce, unemployment, failure, sickness, or loss. Throughout these struggles, trust in God, leaning on Him in good times and in bad times.

Unfortunately, some young people miss this message, trying to cope with life's challenges using self-destructive means. This is not the answer.

'Do not be anxious about anything, but in every situation, by prayer and petition, with thanksgiving, present your requests to God. And the peace of God, which transcends all understanding, will guard your hearts and your minds in Christ Jesus. Finally, brothers and sisters, whatever is true, whatever is noble, whatever is right, whatever is pure, whatever is lovely, whatever is admirable—if anything is excellent or praiseworthy—think about such things.'
Philippians 4:6-8 (NIV)

In Christ Jesus, we can find the cure for our emotional wounds, disappointment, bitterness, and resentment. Jesus can bring peace to our hearts, curing our anxiety, depression, worry, fear, and stress. God can bring us eternal peace and health. Faith in Jesus is what is needed to live a fruitful life in this world and in the world to come. Learn from your pain, and turn it into wisdom. Trust God in all things, and through Him, you will reach your destiny.

Indulgence in Inappropriate Pleasure

The next strategy of the devil is pleasure. We live in a pleasure-seeking world, and in such a world, people regard activities such as drinking, smoking, immoral sexual relations, and gambling as joys of life. These people claim to know what they are doing, and they fail to realise that someone else is willfully influencing them and taking control of their lives. Like a roaring lion seeking someone to devour, Satan is always threatening, attacking, and deceiving people to follow his selfish and destructive desires.

Among the most sought-after pleasures by young people, today is the use of drugs and alcohol. Drugs and alcohol are prevalent in many social gatherings. Frequent use of these substances can lead to addiction. This is evidenced by the many young people roaming the streets of our towns and cities, consuming drugs and alcohol.

There are several reasons that can influence young people to consume drugs and alcohol. These include factors such as family problems and social and political disturbances. Many young people use drugs and alcohol to cope with emotional and psychological pain. However, drugs and alcohol do not solve anything. They only exacerbate existing problems. You cannot address personal issues by avoiding them. Instead, you must approach and confront them with confidence, patience, hope, and faith.

Satan uses these self-destructive practices and habits to keep you under his deceptive detention. He encourages the use of drugs and alcohol to make you believe that life is useless or less enjoyable without them.

The problem is that drugs and alcohol not only destroy the user's body and health but also increase the likelihood that the user will engage in criminal activity. The more frequently you engage in such antisocial activities, the more likely you will be harmed or even killed. And this is the devil's objective. It is essential to know that getting into a lifestyle of drugs and alcohol is one of the significant traps the devil uses to capture the fine and wonderful young people who are supposed to be keys assets for national peace and development.

The next trap the enemy uses against youths is the misuse of sexual pleasure. Sexual pleasure is highly sought after in today's world. Sex is a gift from God, but it should be enjoyed within the circle of marriage. We must follow God's path.

God is our creator. He is the source of all good things. God is the only one who knows what is best for each of us. Living according to His guidance and counsel is what counts most.

When exercised outside of God's plan, sexual pleasure is dangerous, not only for Christian living but also for social life. It can have catastrophic effects on individuals and on society. Engaging in illicit sexual practices can lead to the contraction of sexually transmitted diseases. Other health problems that result from illicit sexual intercourse are emotional and psychological disturbances that may arise as results of unplanned pregnancy and unplanned marriage. Moreover, death from unsafe or self-induced abortion is common. It is one of the leading health conditions facing young people.

What Christian Youths Need to Know

It is essential to know that Satan has all the deceptive techniques he needs to get control of you. These techniques are not new. They have been used for thousands of years. Our Lord, Jesus Christ, faced the same temptation strategies from Satan, but he resisted them all. What an excellent example to follow!

Three Ways in Which Satan Tempts Us

Sin, for many young people today, is a choice, not a compulsion. The tendency to do wrong is so strong that some don't even think rightly about the result of it. Satan has the power to deceive and use individuals for his selfish ambition and desire.

Every child of God must stay on guard, recognising and defending themselves against the enemy's attack. The following are three of the most potent ways in which Satan deceives or tempts people to sin against God and their fellow human beings. These are taken from 1 John 2:16.
- The lust of the flesh
- The lust of the eyes
- The pride of life

Here, John gives us the three main temptations of the world. Every adult in history has been tempted by the lust of the flesh, the lust of the eyes, and the pride of life. It is important to be aware of these temptations that we all face because every sin we commit is believed to be preceded by at least one of these temptations.

The Lust of the Flesh
The lust of the flesh is the temptation to seek physical pleasure through sinful or immoral activity. It involves any type of sinful activity that brings pleasure to the body. Examples include illicit sexual relations, physical violence, and consumption of drugs.

The apostle Paul gives us an excellent example of the 'work of the flesh.' These are the wrong and ungodly activities that we do when we succumb or surrender to the lust of the flesh.

> **The acts of the flesh are obvious: sexual immorality, impurity and debauchery; idolatry and witchcraft; hatred, discord, jealousy, fits of rage, selfish ambition, dissensions, factions and envy; drunkenness, orgies, and the like. I warn you, as I did before, that those who live like this will not inherit the kingdom of God.'**
>
> Galatians 5:19-23 (NIV)

Lust of the Eyes
The lust of the eyes is the temptation to look upon things we shouldn't look upon. In other words, it is to cast our eyes upon things with desire or pleasure, even though God has warned us not to look upon those things. The sin of coveting is a prime example of the result of succumbing to the lust of eyes. 'Thou shall not covet' was the tenth commandment that God gave to the Israelites.

To covet means to have a yearning or a strong desire to have something that rightfully belongs to someone else. Statements such as 'It is not fair that he has such a beautiful wife' are a prime example. Other examples of the lust of the eyes include looking at pornography or desiring someone else's possessions, status, or appearance.

Coveting is the recognition that something sinful has visual appeal and wanting it for the sake of its visual appeal. Consider the example below.

> *'One evening, David got up from his bed and walked around on the roof of the palace. From the roof, he saw a woman bathing. The woman was gorgeous, and David sent someone to find out about her. The man said, "Isn't this Bathsheba, the daughter of Eliam and the wife of Uriah the Hittite?" Then David sent messengers to get her. She came to him, and he slept with her. Then she went back home.'*
>
> 2 Samuel 11:2-4 (NIV)

From the above passage, you can see that David's eyes caused him to sin against God. He lusted after another man's wife. Our eyes are created for sight, and they pass information to the brain. It is up to us to control what our eyes see from the physical environment around us and how our brain interprets such information.

The Pride of Life
The pride of life is the sinful desire for excess greatness or power. Satisfaction is one of the sins that God hates most. It is the sin that made Lucifer, the beautiful angel, turn into Satan, the adversary. The following are the words of Satan himself, who was so filled with pride that he wanted to be God.

> *'I will ascend above the tops of the clouds; I will make myself like the Most High.'*
>
> Isaiah 14:14 (NIV)

The Three Temptations in Action

Every sin we commit involves at least one of the temptations, but it may include all three. Notice how Satan used all three temptations with Eve in the Garden of Eden and with Jesus in the New Testament. Eve succumbed to the temptations. Jesus resisted them.

> *'When the woman saw that the fruit of the tree was good for food* (lust of the flesh) *and pleasing to the eye* (lust of the eyes), *and also desirable for gaining wisdom* (pride of life), *she took some and ate it. She also gave some to her husband, who was with her, and he ate it.'*
>
> Genesis 3:6 (NIV)

In Matthew 4:1-11, Jesus was tempted by Satan. In your own time, read this chapter and see how our good Lord responded to temptation.

What Sin is Not

We have seen how Satan uses his deceptive strategies to make us fall into his trap of loss and death. Now it is important for us to understand what sin is not with regard to the things we say, see, hear, touch, and think.

It is not a sin to enjoy physical pleasure in things in which God allows us to feel joy. God created food to taste delicious. There is nothing wrong with enjoying a delicious meal. We have to eat to live. But gluttony and greediness are sinful and against God.

God also created and designed sex. There is nothing wrong with enjoying sexual intimacy with our spouses, but adultery and fornication are wrong and against God.

It is not a sin to look at the beautiful things God created or things that humans have made from their God-given intellect and wisdom. Things such as stars, mountains, rainbows, oceans, and artworks are beautiful to look at, and this is not a sin. Sin comes when we lustfully look upon things God has commanded us to avoid. When we lustfully look upon things like pornography, other people's spouses, or other people's belongings, it is sinful.

Finally, it is not a sin when we have desire to achieve our dreams. There is nothing wrong with having ambition or desiring to work hard to achieve success. However, when we fail to give glory to God, when we want to be praised for our effort, or when we desire to have power or knowledge for the sake of egotism, we become entangled in the pride of life that could lead to our downfall.

When a person becomes too proud because of achievement, they forget to acknowledge God, and this leads to loss. If you study the book of the first and second Samuel and the book of first and second kings, you will see very quickly that some kings of Israel and Judah—King Saul, King Solomon, King Ahab, and King Ahaziah—disobeyed God. They misused their power, and as a result, they failed and died. King David, King Joash, and King Asa were faithful kings. They refused to be corrupted by power, and they refused to be driven away from obeying God by the pleasure and pride of enjoying the riches of their kingdoms.

It is crucial to keep in mind that pride and boasting did not only make people fail in Biblical times. They have the same effect in our modern world. When we boast or brag about our achievements to others who haven't made it to our level, we prepare ourselves to fail. Do not boast or brag. Be humble, even if you have the reason to boast. The Lord, who sees our hearts from heaven, will lift you up.

How to Respond to Temptations

It is essential to understand that we will all face the lust of the flesh, the lust of the eyes, and the pride of life. However, God promises us that no matter how hard temptations are to resist, He will always provide an escape route. We can always choose obedience over sin. This means that no matter how tempted you may be in a situation, Jesus felt the same way when he was tempted. We should always respond to temptations in the same way that Jesus responded to Satan.

Jesus took the word of God and rebuked Satan. In the same way, we should allow God's words to fill our hearts and minds so that we can rebuke and resist evil. The words of God are powerful and mighty enough to defend us against any attack.

> *'For the word of God is alive and active. Sharper than any double-edged sword, it penetrates even to dividing soul and spirit, joints and marrow; it judges the thoughts and attitudes of the heart.'*
>
> Hebrews 4:12 (NIV)

All Christians can guard themselves against Satan by filling their minds and hearts with the words of God. This will enable them to be fruitful in their faith and to live responsibly in this world. This is an important reason why every young person should remember to serve God throughout their youth. We will discuss this in more detail in our next chapter.

CHAPTER SIX

Remember Your God While Still Young

'Live in such a way that those who know you but don't know God will come to know God because they know you.'
Anonymous

The creationist theory shows us where we came from. Human beings, along with all other living and non-living creatures, came from God, the creator of the universe. God created us out of nothing. This is because He is infinite (unlimited), omnipotent (all-powerful), omnipresent (exists everywhere at the same time), and omniscient (all-knowing).

In His infinite and unlimited wisdom, God created all the living things—human beings, animals, birds, and insects—and non-living things—mountains, rivers, seas, and oceans—that we see around us. God created nothing without purpose. He created everything to fit and live according to the natural laws and principles that guide existence and success. Humans are no different.

You and I were created to function like our creator Himself. We were created to love and care for others and to live morally and spiritually upright. God created man in His image, giving men and women the same life-giving spirit. Trusting God shouldn't just be a part of our daily to-do list. It must be a priority in our lives.

Consider the godly and inspiring life of one young man in the Bible who lived up to his faith: Joseph, the eleventh son of Jacob, who is best known as Israel. This young man, a teenager, succeeded because he always walked with God.

Joseph's Life: An Inspiring Example for Young People

My life changed the first time the Bible introduced to me this great young man. Joseph lived in complete obedience to his God. He was, indeed, a faith hero. We are not going to discuss the whole story of this faithful young man. Instead, we are going to focus on some of the critical aspects of his life. We are going to see what made him so outstanding.

Joseph, from the beginning of his young life, decided to live by faith in God. His faith in God made him smarter than anyone else of his time. There are many qualities we can learn from Joseph and his walk with God.

The qualities I learned from Joseph changed my life for good. They have shaped and redefined my attitude in many ways. The life of this faithful young man revealed to me the source of power and strength to turn life's adversities into opportunities. Joseph's example showed me that I possess an inner power I didn't know I had. This internal power comes from an unshakable faith in God.

Let's explore the life-transforming qualities demonstrated by Joseph and his faith.

Integrity and Faith

Joseph was living in the house of his master, Potiphar, when Potiphar's wife fell in love with him.

> *'Potiphar left everything up to Joseph, and with Joseph there, the only decision he had to make was what he wanted to eat. Joseph was well-built and handsome, and Potiphar's wife soon noticed him. She asked him to make love to her, but he refused and said, "My master isn't worried about anything in his house, because he has placed me in charge of everything he owns. No one in my master's house is more important than I am. The only thing he hasn't given me is you, and that's because you are his wife. I won't sin against God by doing such a terrible thing as this.'*
>
> Genesis 39:6-9 (CEV)

Joseph kept his faith alive. His faith was in action during this tempting situation. Joseph's faith and conviction in the words of God prevented him from agreeing to Potiphar's wife's request.

Temptations to engage in illicit sexual acts are very prevalent for young people today. This is one of the reasons that unplanned pregnancy, abortion, and sexually transmitted diseases are growing problems facing our society.

The good news is that when we, as Christians, exercise obedient faith, as demonstrated by Joseph, we can be safe from destructive behaviour. Genuine faith can help you face life's challenges with hope and confidence. Discipline and self-control are among the most essential qualities one must possess to move through life. Therefore, we must be educated about these qualities. Many of us hold degrees, but while academic papers can help us find work, they can't help us live victoriously and responsibly in this world.

Years ago, when I was studying, my university's campus had a disciplinary committee office, the job of which was to correct, warn, or dismiss students who broke university rules and regulations.

Despite good academic grades, one could not graduate if they had been disciplined by the university for bad behaviour. This is the power of discipline.

> *'Marriage doesn't cure lust; if it did, adultery wouldn't exist. Self-control is still a requirement. Lust doesn't care if you are married or single. You may be Solomon in wisdom or David in praise or Abraham in faith or Joshua in war, but if you are not Joseph in discipline, you will end up like Samson in destruction.'*
>
> Unknown

Discipline and self-control are not only crucial to protecting you from sexual temptations. They can also help and protect you in many other areas of life. Moreover, discipline and self-control can enable you to succeed in life. This is because discipline and self-control that come from faith and hope in God are instrumental in helping you to make good use of your time and talent, helping you to go further in life.

Joseph's God-Given Wisdom

Joseph honoured God with his life. This pleased God much, and He gave Joseph the valuable gift of wisdom. Joseph was so wise that the King told him that no one knew as much as he did.

> *'The king told Joseph, "God is the one who has shown you these things. No one else is as wise as you or knows as much as you do. I am putting you in charge of my palace, and everybody will have to obey you. No one will be over you except me. You are now governor of all Egypt!"'*
>
> Genesis 41:39 (CEV)

The king told young Joseph these things because he had seen him doing extraordinary things. Joseph interpreted the king's dream that made the philosophers of Egypt go almost mad. In addition to this, he suggested the best plan to collect grain from Egypt for all seven years of plentiful harvest. The king's officials and the king himself agreed to Joseph's suggestions.

Joseph was thirty years old when he was made the governor of Egypt and was able to rule as the most influential person after the king. The king relied on him for guidance and direction. The king told Joseph that no one in Egypt would ever be allowed to do anything without his permission. What a blessing!

> *The king told Joseph, "Although I'm king, no one in Egypt is to do anything without your permission."'*
>
> Genesis 41:44 (CEV)

Joseph's Forgiveness and Humility

Joseph demonstrated genuine forgiveness and humility. He did something unexpected for his jealous and selfish brothers. He obeyed Christ's command for his followers to defeat evil with good. Joseph took this principle to heart and lived by it throughout his life.

Uncontrolled jealousy and hatred from his brothers finally culminated in Joseph being thrown into a deep, dark pit, then sold to slavery. But because of the genuine and faith in God that filled his heart, Joseph forgave those who had harmed him.

If God's words hadn't filled Joseph's heart and mind, he would have thought differently. He would have felt discouraged and hopeless and may have harmed himself. But in spite of all that had happened to him, Joseph didn't lose his faith in God. He didn't ask God what the meaning behind his dreams was. Joseph didn't blame God for the troubles he was experiencing. Instead, he believed that God could do what seemed impossible and provide a way out of any situation. What genuine faith!

> *The ability to show courage in the face of adversity; show self-restraint in the face of temptation, choose happiness in the face of hurt, show character in the face of despair, and see opportunity in the face of obstacles are all valuable traits to possess.*
>
> Shiv Khera

Joseph's Unconditional Love

A thorough understanding of the concept of love is fundamental. Unconditional love is a command given by God to those who follow him. This kind of love is permanent and unbreakable.

Joseph and many other faith heroes have taught us about unconditional love. *Agape* love is the kind of love that teaches and commands us to love and pray for our enemies and those who have hurt us, and this is exactly what Joseph did for his brothers. But one cannot possess or enact this love outside of Christ. When we honour God with our lives, we have the map and compass we need to help us navigate our way through life properly. We have qualities of love, discipline, self-control, humility, kindness, positivity, and self-esteem. There are situations in life in which forgiveness may seem impossible. All you may want to do is retaliate, but retaliation doesn't solve any problems, and it doesn't teach any lessons. Only the genuine forgiveness that comes from unconditional love can do these things.

In Greek tradition, love exists in four types. *Agape*, as discussed above, is divine, unconditional love. The three remaining types are *eros*, *storge*, and *philia*. All of these types of love are temporary and can thus change or end at any time.

Eros is sensual love. It is based on the five physical senses. If someone makes you feel good or if they are pretty or handsome, you may feel love for them. This love is self-centred and seeks to gratify itself. When it is no longer gratified, it ends and dies. It is based on self-benefit.

Storge is familial love. It is love that exists between parents and children and between brothers and sisters. It ends when family members fail to fulfil their roles and responsibilities to one another or take separate paths.

Philia is the love that exists between friends. It is conditional and temporary, ending with acts of selfishness, remoteness, or lack of support.

You may be experiencing difficulties or painful circumstances in your life. But despite the source of such challenges, be like Joseph. Joseph was humble in the face of adversity. He was cautious and careful, and he didn't give the devil the chance to plant seeds of negativity or retaliation in his mind. He let go of the disappointments and frustrations that resulted from the devil's schemes against him. He never lost his faith in God.

Just like Joseph, you have the capacity within you to forgive whoever has hurt you. You have the potential within you to discover and release your inner power and strength to make today's pain become tomorrow's opportunity.

Serving your creator while still young, is like opening a bank account. The more you deposit, the more you will gain. Fill your heart and mind with faith and obedience to God, and you will receive abundantly in return. I challenge you to have unmovable and victorious faith in God, for this is the only way to discover your true self and become an ideal human being.

CHAPTER SEVEN

THE SUCCESS FORMULA

'I can do all this through him who gives me strength.'
Philippians 4:13 (NIV)

God created us to succeed in life. It saddens God's heart to see us fail and live purposeless lives. To reach our true potential, we must adhere to the spiritual and divine principles that regulate and guide us to succeed in life.

Man as a created being is of two kinds: the inner man and the outer man. The inner man is made up of the spirit and soul that lives in each of us. The outer man is the physical body. Understanding the two states of man is the key to success. Your inner man is the real you. It is one that determines your success and failure in life, depending on what and how often you feed it.

The problem today is that most people take good care of their physical bodies but do not do the same for their inner selves. We should take good care of our physical bodies, but they shouldn't be our priority. Our primary focus should be on what's inside. Real success comes from within. Consider the short story below.

There was a man who made his living selling balloons. He had balloons of many different colours — red, yellow, blue, and green. Whenever business was slow, he would release a helium-filled balloon into the air. When the children saw the balloon go up, they all wanted one. They would hurry to him and buy a balloon, and his sales would go up. The man continued to release balloons whenever sales slowed down. One day, the balloon man felt someone tugging at his jacket. He turned around.

A little boy asked, "If you release a black balloon, would that also fly?"

Moved by the boy's concern, the man replied gently, "Son, it is not the colour of the balloon. It is what is inside that makes it go up."[6]

Our attitude is responsible for our potential and success in life. In fact, our attitude is the highest pillar upon which our success is anchored. Now, if attitude is of such importance, where can we learn it?

First and foremost, we must understand that we are not born with a positive or negative attitude. It is something we pick up and learn throughout our lives. Several factors determine our attitude. These include our environment, our life experience, and our education, formal or informal. When imparted appropriately, training can help us develop the knowledge and skills required to broaden our minds and challenge our thinking and reasoning capacity.

The True Source of a Positive Attitude that Leads to Success

Having a positive attitude is the basis for success in every area of life. To have that basis for success, we must consult the constitution of life:

---

6   Adapted from *YOU CAN WIN*, a revised edition by SHIV KHERA, p.2

the Bible. The Bible is not just a book. It is the book of books written by the Holy Spirit. It is centuries old, but it remains as relevant today as it was all those years ago. The words of the Bible will live on, even when we are gone.

The Bible's counsel and guidance are vital for our existence. The Bible reveals the purpose of God for man, and it shows the answers to the three most common questions of life: Where did I come from? Why am I here? Where am I going after death?

'THE BIBLE LIVES [7]
Generation follows generation — yet it lives.
Nation and kingdom rise and fall — yet it lives.
Kings, dictators, presidents come and go — yet it lives.
Hated, despised, cursed — yet it lives.
Doubted, suspected, and criticised — yet it lives.
Scoffed by scorners — yet it lives.
Exaggerated by fanatics — yet it lives.
Misconstrued and misstated — yet it lives.
Yet it lives — as a lamp to our feet.
Yet it lives — as a light to our path.
Yet it lives — as the gate to heaven.
Yet it lives — as a standard for childhood.
Yet it lives — as a guide for youth.
Yet it lives — as an inspiration for martyred.
Yet it lives — as a comfort for aged.
Yet it lives — as food for the hungry.
Yet it lives — as water for the thirsty.
Yet it lives — as rest for the weary.
Yet it lives — as light for the heathen.

---

[7] Adapted from *The Evangelism Handbook of New Testament* by Phil Sanders, printed Dec 8, 2009, p.46

Yet it lives — as salvation for the sinner.
Yet it lives — as grace for the Christian.
To know is to love it.
To love it is to accept it.
To accept it means life eternal.'

In a nutshell, the Bible is the book of life that teaches us not only how to succeed but also how to handle success. It is the only right source from which one can draw information and develop a better and more positive attitude. Let us consider the following Bible passages that promise us success.

> *'Blessed is the man who does not walk in the counsel of the wicked or stand in the way of sinners or sit in the seat of mockers. But his delight in the law of the LORD, and his law he meditates day and night. He is like a tree planted by streams of water, which yields its fruit in season and whose leaf does not wither. Whatever he does prospers.'*
>
> Psalm 1:1-3 (NIV)

> *'How can a young person stay on the path of purity? By living according to your word.'*
>
> Psalm 119:9 (NIV)

> *'Be strong and courageous, because you will lead these people to inherit the land I swore to their ancestors to give them. "Be strong and very courageous. Be careful to obey all the law my servant Moses gave you; do not turn from it to the right or to the left, that you may be successful wherever you go. Keep this Book of the Law*

always on your lips; meditate on it day and night, so that you may be careful to do everything written in it. Then you will be prosperous and successful.'

Joshua 1:6-9 (NIV)

From the above passages, it is clear that we, as human beings, and particularly as young people, can become successful and prosperous when knowledge and wisdom from the Bible are given priority in our lives.

For example, people like Paul, David, and Joshua lived in faithful obedience to God. They became successful and prosperous in their lifetimes, and more importantly, they rejoice in the kingdom of God afterlife.

'A thorough knowledge of the Bible is worth more than a college education.'

Theodore Roosevelt

Other examples of Bible-inspired people who have influenced our world are Mother Teresa; Francis of Assisi, Italy; and John Wesley of England. There is no one who has not heard of the work of Mother Teresa. She spent her life caring for the wretched and the poor. She said her work was based on the words of Christ in the Gospel of Matthew, chapter twenty-four, where Christ said that we serve and minister to him when we care for the hungry, the poor, and the naked.

When we consider the above examples and many others, we can see that the Bible can tremendously help every person succeed in life, regardless of academic qualifications. How? The Bible points you to God, your source, and helps you direct, focus, and live your life with faith in Him, the creator of heaven and earth.

Faith and trust in the Lord make us hopeful, fearless, and courageous as we deal with day-to-day circumstances and hardships. They help us face life's challenges and adversities with courage and hope, knowing that one day, things will turn to joy.

On top of that, faith enables us to succeed because it is the driving force of vision. It keeps us strong and moving forward, even when we are faced with seemingly impossible obstacles. By faith, you can do anything. This is important because doubt and fear of failure are thieves that steal our hope and courage to trust in the Lord, who strengthens us to do anything. One writer refers to such negative factors (of mind and emotion) collectively as 'diseases of attitude.' The list of these factors, according to him, is as follows:

Self-pity
Feeling sorry for yourself won't help you to live a better life. Self-pity paralyses you and leaves you unable to take any action towards improving your situation. There is a distinct difference between acknowledging that you are not where you would like to be and feeling sorry for yourself. One leads to doing something about the problem, while the other leads to the problem worsening.

Neglect
A week of neglect can cost you a year of repair. Neglecting to care for your financial situation can lead to a situation that may be difficult to climb out of. Neglecting your physical health increases the likelihood of losing it over time. Neglecting your relationships may mean losing them altogether. Pay attention to the things that are important in your life. Failing to do so can have disastrous results.

Indifference
You are neither hot nor cold. You don't care at all. You are drifting through life with a directionless sail that will lead to an undetermined destination. You can't drift your way into prosperity. To be successful

in anything, you have to care about it. If you are inspired, you will have the energy to move mountains. If you are desperate, you will have the energy to fight your way out of difficult circumstances. But if you are indifferent, you are destined to live in metaphorical limbo for the rest of your life.

Indecision

You can't make up your mind as to what to do with your life. You struggle to choose a path that's right for you. Indecisiveness keeps you in precisely the same position you have always been in. Leaders have to be able to make decisions, and if you are not able to come to a decision quickly, you can't be considered a leader. A life of adventure is filled with decisions. The decisions that turn out to be incorrect help to teach you new perspectives and provide you with valuable experiences that can inform future decisions.

Doubt

There are several types of uncertainty, but self-doubt is the most damaging. You doubt if you are good enough, smart enough, or talented enough. You question if you can reach your goals, and even when you find success, you doubt if it will last. If you don't believe in yourself, the game is over before you begin playing. Success comes from faith and self-confidence. Self-worth is the beginning of progress.

Worrying

Incessant worry has a negative impact on your mental state and your physical health. Worrying doesn't solve anything. Give it up. Eradicate it from your life completely. Removing worry is a liberating experience. It doesn't remove difficulty, challenges, or obstacles from your life, but it makes you more capable of facing them.

Over-caution
You are afraid to take risks. You say to yourself, "What if I try and fail?" or "What if it doesn't work?" You highlight the risk instead of looking at the reward. The penalty for not trying at all outweighs the penalty for trying and failing. You should fear risking your sanity for a life of presumed safety and security. You should fear risking living a life filled with regret. Either you join the game or stand on the sidelines and watch the winners play. The choice is yours.

Pessimism
The glass is always half empty. You go out of your way to find the negative in every situation. Spending your whole life looking for reasons why things won't work is a surefire way to be unhappy. Your mind is like a field, and your thoughts are like seeds. Your mind doesn't care what you plant; it will grow whatever seeds you decide to sow, and when harvest time comes, you will reap what you have sown in abundance. Poor thinking habits lead to a poor existence.

Closed-mindedness
You think you know everything. You are the type of person who loves to spout your opinions but doesn't want to hear anyone else's. You think you have life all figured out. Epictetus said, 'It is impossible to begin to learn that which one thinks one already knows.' Instead of having a know-it-all approach to life, become more curious. Open your mind to new ways of thinking, new types of people, and new experiences. It is nearly impossible to live a great life with a closed mind and a hardened heart.

Complaining
Whining, crying, moaning, and groaning. It goes by several monikers. If you don't stop complaining, you cannot have a great life.

Complaining kills dreams with assassin-like efficiency. You complain about the weather, your job, your partner, and your kids; you complain about everything. Stop it. Don't cry about your life. Do something about it. Have faith in God. Be positive and courageous spiritually, mentally, and emotionally as you strive to achieve your dreams.

A positive attitude is the foundation of success. A person with a positive attitude and positive self-esteem is less likely to suffer from so-called diseases of attitude. It is important to remember that success is not ahead of you. It is trapped inside of you.

Success comes the moment you win the battle against negative thinking habits. These are what hold us back from achieving our potential. The good news is that God when trusted and honoured with our lives, can open the door of success for us. He is the vine, and we are the branches. Therefore, if we want to be successful, we must make sure that we always remain connected with Christ in faith. This does not just mean believing that there is a God, as most of us do. Instead, it is an actionable faith. It is unshakable and obedient faith that unlocks blessings and wisdom from the Father above.

Success is not luck; it is the result of dedication and discipline that comes from faith and hope in God. It was not an easy road for Joseph to become a leader of Egypt. It was not a comfortable journey for David to be the justest ruler the world had ever had. It was not an easy road for Esther to become a respected queen who saved her nation. It was not an easy road for Martin Luther King or Gandhi to continue preaching love and non-violence despite the fact that they were often threatened with swords, bullets, and death. Lastly, it was not an easy thing for Mandela to achieve the non-racially divided South Africa we see today. God, when genuinely trusted and depended upon, rewards His faithful servants not only with wealth and health but also with glory and honour.

Conclusion

Young people have the ability and capacity to become the agents of change and development they were born to be. The truth of the matter is that you must use your time wisely and responsibly while you have the breath of life in your body. Youth is the right time to begin the adventure of self-discovery. This is important in enabling you to leave behind the kind of legacy that the next generation can be proud of.

Young people can achieve their goals, becoming people of worth, value, and responsibility, by acquiring the right tool to enrich and boost their mental, spiritual, emotional, and psychological energy. This powerful tool is education.

James T. Adams once said that there are two types of education: one that teaches us how to live and another that teaches us how to make a living. This is the power of education. This concept of two educations was referred to by Dr Martin Luther King Jr when he delivered his Nobel Peace Prize speech in Oslo, Norway, in 1963:

'I have the audacity to believe that people everywhere can have three meals a day for the bodies; education and culture for their minds; and dignity, equality, and freedom for their spirits.'

Martin Luther King Jr

People with no proper education, the type that teaches how to make a living, may hardly have meals three times per day. A lack of knowledge can make it hard for people to get food on the table. A lack of proper education can also make people unwilling or reluctant to accept love and unity. This is demonstrated, for example, by widespread images of people being undermined instead of being treated with respect and dignity; inequalities and rifts between various communities, ethnic groups, and societies; and political leaders who often treat their citizens harshly, thus denying them freedom. All of these acts depict the social and the political messes of our time, which result from the insufficiency of moral education—the one that teaches us how to live.

Education that teaches us how to live is more important than that which teaches us how to make a living. Our actions in life are usually influenced by choices that come from our inner selves. Knowing and understanding how to live with ourselves can help us to live peacefully with each other.

This is why social responsibility should be a priority of every young person, irrespective of gender, socioeconomic status, or political status. We must learn to depend on each other. We must learn to admit that others' happiness and wellbeing rely on us. We, as young people, should always strive to direct our thoughts and actions towards making our communities, our nations, and our world better places to live.

For all these things to happen as desired, we must all realise that we come to this earth for a purpose. Discovering our purpose for living should be a turning point for personal betterment. Living as people with assignments entrusted to us by our creator could make our world a haven for all.

In the process of becoming who we are or who we want to become, there are a lot of distracting and tough things to deal with. These are painful circumstances that are often used by the devil to distract us. Satan uses traps of pain and pleasure to corrupt and discourages us. But a genuine faith in God, who holds the key to our existence and success, is the solid ground that can keep us in the right position in defiance of temptations and challenges.

Faith helps us do and overcome things we can't do or resist on our own. It is our source of strength and hopes to move what seems unmovable. This is why the Bible tells us to live not by sight but by faith. God is our source, and our success depends on Him.

No matter how big the obstacle in our way, God is in control of all things. He is bigger, greater, and mightier than anything else. Always depend on Him, for He has all the answers. Have trust in Him that you will be saved, and seek His knowledge and wisdom to succeed and live a fruitful and fulfilled life of purpose and victory. Praise God! Amen.

About the Author

GATLUAK DANG THOAT is a nationalist and a motivated young writer born to a family of six children, of which he is the third. He was born on 15 October 1994 in a small village called Ngueny in Nasir, Upper Nile State, South Sudan. Gatluak attended primary education in three primary schools: Seventh Days Adventists (SDA) Church Primary School, Both Diu Junior School, and Good Shepherd Junior and Secondary School, Malakal.

After finishing his primary education, he joined High School at Good Shepherd Secondary School (GSSS) of Presbyterian Church in Malakal. Then he obtained his Bachelor of Science (BSc) from Mizan-Tepi University, Ethiopia. Gatluak also took several Bible correspondence courses with International Bible Teaching Ministries (IBTMinisteries), World Bible School (WBS), and Bold Christian University (BCU), USA. Currently, Gatluak is studying a Bachelor of Arts (BA) in Developmental Studies.

In addition to his hard work as a Registered Clinical Midwifery Practitioner (RCMP), who promotes, prevents, and treats maternal and neonatal health conditions, Gatluak decided to remain socially active by sharing his God-given talent and gift with and for the world.

ABOUT THE AUTHOR

He has a passion and conviction in his heart to work for peace, forgiveness, reconciliation, and non-violent conflict resolution, nationally and internationally.

Gatluak is a humble, compassionate, and loving person who practises what he writes. His mission is to inspire and transform communities to become better and more enlightened. He achieves this through writing, speaking, mediation, and counselling in areas of peace-building, conflict prevention and management, youth coaching, and leadership.

Age doesn't make a person mentally, emotionally, socially, or spiritually mature or wise. But knowing and understanding who you are, why you were born, and what you can do for yourself and others is the key to living a happy and fulfilled life. Young people are the agents of change to make our world a better place to live.

This is what Confucius had in mind when he said:

"To put the world in order, we must first put the nation in order; to put the nation in order, we must first put the family in order; to put the family in order, we must first cultivate our personal life; we must set our hearts right."

Young people are, indeed, the most valuable assets of every society. When properly educated, they can create a peaceful environment for themselves and those around them.

This handbook has been written to inspire young people, enabling them to realise their innate worth and true potential so that they can live better, more fruitful lives of faith, hope, and success.

This handbook is also appropriate for use by parents, teachers, pastors, governments, and NGOs.

Lightning Source UK Ltd.
Milton Keynes UK
UKHW010800290720
367358UK00001B/285